Rose Elliot's Book of Beans and Lentils

Rose Elliot is the author of several bestselling cookbooks, and is renowned for her practical and creative approach. She writes regularly for the *Vegetarian* and has contributed to national newspapers and magazines as well as broadcasting on radio and television. She is married and has three children.

Other titles available in the series

Rose Elliot's Book of
Beans and Lentils

Fontana Paperbacks

First published by Fontana Paperbacks 1984
Second impression May 1985

Copyright © Rose Elliot 1984

Set in 10 on 11pt Linotron Plantin
Drawings by Vana Haggerty
except pages 6–7 by Ken Lewis
Made and printed in Great Britain by
William Collins Sons & Co. Ltd, Glasgow

Introduction

Wonderfully cheap, colourful and tasty, dried beans, peas and lentils, known collectively as 'pulses', are satisfying ingredients to use. They're packed with protein and have been used for centuries as natural 'meat-extenders' – or instead of meat – throughout the world.

Not nearly as 'fattening' as people think, being only around 80 calories an ounce, dry weight (160–240 calories an average serving), pulses are fun to cook because they absorb flavours and are extremely versatile. They make excellent warming soups and main courses, refreshing salads, tangy dips and first courses, tasty snacks – and even a moist and delicious protein-rich tea bread!

Don't let the thought of the preparation put you off: it's extremely simple and straightforward as you'll see. But first, here is an alphabetical guide to pulses:

TYPES OF PULSES AVAILABLE

1 Aduki beans Small, reddish brown beans, round with a small point at one end. Have a pleasant, slightly sweet flavour. Good in vegetable stews (see page 45).

ADUKI BEANS

BLACK BEANS

BLACK-EYED BEANS

BORLOTTI BEANS

BRITISH FIELD BEANS

BROAD BEAN

BUTTER BEAN

CANNELLINI BEAN

FUL MEDAMES BEAN

HARICOT BEAN

MUNG
BEANS

PINTO
BEANS

RED KIDNEY
BEANS

SOYA
BEANS

CHICK
PEAS

DRIED
PEAS

SPLIT
PEAS

CONTINENTAL
LENTILS

SPLIT
RED
LENTILS

LIMA
BEAN

FLAGEOLET
BEAN

7

2 Black beans A type of kidney bean, a little larger than red kidney beans, shiny black in colour. Have a rich flavour and pleasant, mealy texture. Delicious in vegetable casseroles and salads; can be used instead of red kidney beans in any recipe.

3 Black-eyed peas Sometimes called black-eyed beans or cowpeas. About the same size as haricot beans, beige-coloured with a black spot or 'eye'. They cook quickly and have a pleasant, slightly sweet flavour.

4 Field beans One of the cheapest beans, which can be grown in gardens and allotments in temperate climates. They have a tough outer skin so need chopping in a food processor or strong blender to break this down and release the pleasant, earthy flavour. Excellent in a dip (page 32), and as burgers (page 31).

5 Butter beans One of the largest beans, flattish, kidney-shaped and creamy white in colour. They absorb flavours particularly well and are useful for making pâtés (page 25), or combined with tasty vegetables and spices (pages 24 and 26).

6 Cannellini beans White kidney-shaped beans, a little larger than red kidney beans, and a member of the same family. Pleasant flavour and texture; can be used in place of haricot, butter or red kidney beans.

7 Chick peas Look like small hazel nuts, beige in colour, cooking to a darker gold. Have a particularly delicious flavour and are excellent in salads and casseroles, also in dips, such as hummus (page 37), and in crisp croquettes (page 30).

8 Continental lentils Large, flat and lens-shaped, these vary in colour from light greenish beige to brown. They retain their shape after cooking and are excellent with spices and warm bread or rice (page 42), or made into tasty non-meat burgers (page 23).

9 Flageolet beans Have an attractive pale green colour, slim shape and delicate flavour when cooked. They make an excellent salad, particularly when combined with other pale green vegetables such as avocado (page 35); they also make a pretty pale green soup (page 33).

10 Haricot beans These small, oval white beans belong to the kidney bean family. Probably best known in the form of 'baked beans', they have a delicious slightly sweet flavour and mealy texture. Try them as Boston baked beans (page 21), in a tasty flan (page 36), or as a salad, following the recipe on page 19, but using only haricot beans, and plenty of chopped fresh herbs.

11 Mung beans Are the small, round green beans from which bean sprouts are produced. Delicious cooked with rice and spices in the traditional Indian dish, khitchari (page 38).

12 Peas These are whole dried peas and look like wizened versions of fresh peas. They cook to the familiar 'mushy peas' and make a cheap and filling winter vegetable or soup: see page 46 or follow the recipe for lentil soup on page 41, but leave out the apple and spices and flavour with some chopped mint.

13 Pinto beans Pinto means 'speckled' and these beans are creamy coloured with brown specks. They are a type of kidney bean and can be used in any recipe calling for red kidney beans or haricot beans.

They have a delicate, slightly sweet flavour and can be made into a moist tea bread (page 49).

14 Puy lentils Sometimes called brown lentils, these are dark brown or reddish brown lentils, smaller than continental lentils and with a more intense flavour. They are interchangeable with continental lentils and make excellent burgers (page 23).

15 Red kidney beans Rich red in colour and with the characteristic kidney shape, these have a delicious mealy texture and an excellent flavour. They combine well with rice (page 51), and are widely used in South America and the West Indies in recipes such as refried beans (page 53). For red bean salad, follow the recipe on page 19, using all red kidney beans and adding a tablespoon of tomato ketchup to the dressing.

16 Split red lentils These are lentils which have had the outer skin removed and are bright orange-red in colour. Easy to buy at any supermarket, they have a pleasant savoury flavour and cook quickly to a purée. Excellent made into soup (page 41), rissoles (page 44), savoury spread (page 43), or spicy dal (page 29).

17 Soya beans Small, round and yellowish in colour. The most protein-rich pulse, but not particularly useful because of their strong flavour and long cooking time.

18 Split peas Bright green or yellow in colour, these, like split red lentils, have had their outer skin removed. Undercook them slightly so that they still hold their shape and mix them with dressing to make an unusual salad (page 59), or cook them to a purée and make traditional and comforting pease pudding (page 47), or tasty split peas with fennel seeds (page 57).

(page 47) (page 57)

CHOOSING PULSES

Although pulses will keep for many years, they become harder and drier with time. So for best results buy fresh stock from a shop with a rapid turnover and store carefully in a screwtop jar or airtight cannister, using up each batch before topping up with the next. There is a new season of pulses every autumn.

EQUIPMENT

The equipment required for cooking pulses is simple and basic. A large sieve or colander is useful for washing the pulses and a large saucepan in which to soak and cook them. As most pulses take quite a long time to cook, a pressure cooker saves time and fuel and a slow cooker can also be used. A food mill, liquidizer or food processor is needed for puréeing the pulses to make soups and dips, and essential for preparing field beans.

11

1 Washing

Many pulses are cleaned before packing, but they are sometimes dusty and occasionally there are small pieces of grit or wood with them. I have found this especially with brown lentils and chick peas and it's a wise precaution to spread these out on a large white plate or tray and sort them through carefully, removing any foreign bodies. Then put the pulses into a large colander or sieve and wash them under cold water, moving them about with your fingers as you do so.

2 Soaking

Most pulses need soaking before cooking. This is unnecessary for split red lentils, and optional for the other types of lentils, small green mung beans, split peas and black-eyed peas, although soaking these does reduce their cooking time and helps them to cook more evenly.

Put the pulses into a large saucepan and cover them with their height again in cold water. Either leave them to soak for 6–8 hours, or bring them to the boil, boil for 2 minutes, then remove from heat and soak for 45–60 minutes.

3 Rinsing

Next, whether you've done the long cold soak or the short hot soak, the pulses should be turned into a colander and rinsed thoroughly under cold water. This helps to remove some of the sugars, called oligosaccharides, which can make pulses indigestible.

4 Basic Cooking

Put the rinsed pulses into a large saucepan with a generous covering of fresh water. A homemade unsalted stock can be used instead of water, but do not use a salty stock or add salt, as this can toughen the outside of the beans and prevent them from cooking properly. Bring the water to the boil and allow to boil rapidly for 10 minutes. This destroys any toxins which may be present in some types of bean (especially red kidney beans), making them perfectly safe to eat. After this initial boiling the pulses can be incorporated with other ingredients and cooked slowly, or they can be gently simmered on their own until tender and then mixed with other ingredients. See table for cooking times (page 14), but remember that these can vary a little from batch to batch (particularly chick peas).

Using a pressure cooker This reduces the cooking time by about two-thirds. Boil the pulses for 10 minutes as usual, then cook at 6.7 kg (15 lb) pressure for a third of the usual time given in the chart. Some of the pulses, particularly lentils, tend to 'froth up' when they come to the boil, and this can clog the valve of the pressure cooker. You can avoid this by adding 2 tablespoons of oil to the cooking water.

Using a slow cooker This is an economical way to cook pulses but it is

13

important to boil the pulses vigorously for 10 minutes before transferring them to the slow cooker. Pulses which normally take 1–1½ hours to cook need 2–3 hours in a slow cooker with the heat set at 'low'.

SOAKING AND COOKING TIMES

	cold soak	hot soak	average cooking time
Aduki beans	6–8 hours	45–60 minutes	1–1½ hours
Black beans	6–8 hours	45–60 minutes	1–1½ hours
Black-eyed peas	6–8 hours	45–60 minutes	25–30 minutes
	unsoaked	unsoaked	35–45 minutes
Butter beans	6–8 hours	45–60 minutes	45–60 minutes
Cannellini beans	6–8 hours	45–60 minutes	1–1½ hours
Chick peas	6–8 hours	45–60 minutes	1–2 hours
Field beans	6–8 hours	45–60 minutes	30–60 minutes
Flageolet beans	6–8 hours	45–60 minutes	30–60 minutes
Haricot beans	6–8 hours	45–60 minutes	1–1½ hours
Lentils			
Continental	6–8 hours	45–60 minutes	25–30 minutes
	unsoaked	unsoaked	1–1½ hours
Puy	6–8 hours	45–60 minutes	25–30 minutes
	unsoaked	unsoaked	1–1½ hours

	cold soak	hot soak	average cooking time
Split red	unsoaked	unsoaked	20–30 minutes
Mung beans	6–8 hours	45–60 minutes	25–30 minutes
	unsoaked	unsoaked	30–40 minutes
Peas, whole	6–8 hours	45–60 minutes	45–60 minutes
Pinto beans	6–8 hours	45–60 minutes	1–1½ hours
Red kidney beas	6–8 hours	45–60 minutes	1–1¼ hours
Soya beans	6–8 hours	45–60 minutes	1–3 hours
Split peas	6–8 hours	45–60 minutes	25–30 minutes
	unsoaked	unsoaked	45–60 minutes

5 Flavouring and serving

Pulses are simple to cook, but it's the flavouring and presentation which make all the difference to the attractiveness of the finished dish. Butter and well-flavoured vegetable oils – in particular olive oil – enhance them greatly, as do small quantities of cream. Strongly flavoured vegetables, such as onions, garlic, celery, mushrooms and tomatoes, also go particularly well with pulses and so do some fruits, particularly sharp apples, pineapple, dried apricots, raisins or sultanas and also lemon juice. Do not add acid fruits, or tomatoes, until after the pulses have softened – the pulses may toughen.

Perhaps more than anything else, herbs and spices make all the difference to the appeal of the finished dish. It is surprising what the addition of a bay leaf or bouquet garni to the cooking water of any of the pulses will do for the flavour. The bouquet garni herbs are bay leaf, thyme, parsley and marjoram, and these can be used together or individually. Other useful herbs are mint and oregano, while of the spices, fennel, cumin, coriander, cinnamon and cadamom seeds are particularly good ones to have; also chilli powder, paprika, cloves, curry powder or paste, and turmeric. Grated fresh ginger root, with its delicious citrus-like flavour, also comes in handy.

Pulse dishes look attractive served simply, in chunky pottery, with garnishes such as triangles of crisp toast or fried bread, raw onion or tomato rings, lemon wedges or chopped parsley.

6 Storing cooked pulses

Drained, cooked pulses will keep for several days in a covered container in the fridge and they also freeze well. It is often worth cooking a double batch, using half and freezing the rest.

Many made-up pulse dishes also freeze well and these recipes are marked Ⓕ. Freeze the dishes after cooking unless stated otherwise and thaw before reheating. Rissoles and fritters should be open-freezed then packed in polythene bags. They can be fried while still frozen.

Aduki Bean, Carrot and Ginger Stir-fry

The beans for this stir-fry are cooked in advance – and if you do an extra batch they can be kept in the freezer for another occasion. Serve with fluffy brown rice and a side salad.

SERVES 4

1 onion, sliced
4 tablespoons oil
700 g (1½ lb) carrots, thinly sliced
1 tablespoon grated fresh ginger
125 g (4 oz) aduki beans, soaked, cooked and drained

300 ml (½ pint) water or stock
bunch of spring onions, chopped
salt and pepper
sugar

Fry the onion in a large saucepan for 4–5 minutes, until beginning to soften, then add the carrots and ginger and stir-fry for a further 3–4 minutes. Add the aduki beans and water, cover and leave to simmer gently for 10–15 minutes, until the carrots are just tender. Stir in the spring onions. Season with salt and pepper and a dash of sugar if necessary.

Black Bean Moussaka

SERVES 6 (F)

1 large aubergine
salt
1 onion, chopped
1 garlic clove, crushed
2 tablespoons olive oil
3 tomatoes, skinned and
    chopped
1 tablespoon tomato purée

225 g (8 oz) black beans, cooked
    and drained
1 teaspoon cinnamon
3–4 tablespoons red wine
freshly ground black pepper
400 ml (¾ pint) cheese sauce
75 g (3 oz) grated cheese

Slice the aubergine thinly, sprinkle with salt, leave for 30 minutes, then rinse and dry. Set oven to 180°C (350°F), gas mark 4. Fry onion and garlic in the oil for 10 minutes, then add tomatoes, purée, beans, spices, wine and seasoning. Mix well, mashing beans a little. Layer aubergine and bean mixture in shallow ovenproof dish. Pour sauce over top, sprinkle with cheese. Bake for 1 hour.

Black and White Bean Salad
with Lemon Thyme

Bean salads are especially attractive when made from two or more contrasting beans and this is a particularly pleasant combination.

SERVES 4–6 (F)

125 g (4 oz) black beans
125 g (4 oz) cannellini beans
½ teaspoon dry mustard
½ teaspoon soft brown sugar
4 teaspoons wine vinegar

4 tablespoons olive oil
1 tablespoon chopped lemon
   thyme (or other fresh herbs as
   available)
salt and pepper

Soak, rinse and cook the beans as described on page 12, keeping the two types separate. Don't let them overcook: they are best when they still have a little 'bite' to them. Put the mustard, sugar and vinegar into a large bowl and mix together, then add the oil, herbs, hot beans and seasoning. Mix gently, then leave until cool, stirring occasionally. Serve cold, in a shallow bowl.

Black-eyed Peas with Apples, Sultanas, Brazil Nuts and Curried Mayonnaise

A complete-meal salad with a delightful mixture of flavours and textures. Serve with warm wholewheat rolls.

SERVES 4

175 g (6 oz) black-eyed peas, cooked and drained
1 large sweet apple, diced
1 tablespoon lemon juice
75 g (3 oz) sultanas
75 g (3 oz) brazil nuts, roughly chopped

2 tablespoons mayonnaise
2 tablespoons natural yoghurt
1–2 teaspoons curry paste
salt and pepper
crisp lettuce leaves
chopped chives

Put the beans into a large bowl. Sprinkle the apple with lemon juice, then add to the beans, together with the sultanas and nuts. Mix mayonnaise and yoghurt together in a separate small bowl, adding curry paste to taste. Gently stir this dressing into the bean mixture; season. Serve on a base of crisp lettuce leaves with some chives snipped on top.

Boston Baked Beans

Although most recipes for these homemade baked beans use uncooked beans, I find cooking the beans before adding the other ingredients gives a better flavour and makes the beans more tender. Good with warm crusty wholewheat bread or jacket potatoes.

SERVES 4 (F)

1 onion, chopped
1 tablespoon oil
2 tcaspoons dry mustard
4 teaspoons brown sugar
2 teaspoons black treacle

1½ teaspoons salt
3 tablespoons tomato purée
350 g (12 oz) haricot beans,
   soaked and cooked
1–2 tablespoons lemon juice

Set oven to 275°F (140°C), gas mark 1. Fry the onion in the oil for 10 minutes, then put into an ovenproof casserole large enough to hold the beans. Mix in the mustard, sugar, treacle, salt and tomato purée. Drain beans, reserving 150 ml (¼ pint) liquid. Gently stir beans and liquid into tomato mixture. Cover and bake for about 1 hour, stirring occasionally. Add lemon juice, check seasoning.

BROW
LENT

Brown Lentil Burgers

These lentil burgers are cheap, tasty and healthy. I like them with salad and a dollop of mayonnaise or a yoghurt and chive dressing. They are also good on warm rolls with pickles.

SERVES 4

350 g (12 oz) continental or puy lentils, soaked and drained
1 bay leaf
1 onion, peeled and finely chopped
2 tablespoons wholewheat flour
1 tablespoon tomato purée
4 tablespoons chopped parsley
salt and pepper
wholewheat flour for coating
oil for shallow frying

Put the lentils and bay leaf into a large saucepan, cover with a generous amount of water and bring to the boil. Boil for 10 minutes, then turn heat down and leave lentils to simmer gently for 45–60 minutes, until tender. Drain and remove bay leaf. Add remaining ingredients to lentils and mix well, mashing the lentils a little. Form into burgers, coat with flour, shallow-fry over a moderate heat until crisp on both sides.

Butter Beans with Apricots, Cinnamon and Almonds

An unusual sweet and sour mixture with a Middle Eastern flavour. Delicious as an accompaniment to curry or as a main dish with fluffy boiled rice and a green salad.

SERVES 2–3 AS A MAIN DISH, 4–6 AS A SIDE DISH (F)

1 onion, chopped
2 tablespoons oil
1½–2 teaspoons cinnamon
125 g (4 oz) butter beans, cooked and drained
125 g (4 oz) dried apricots, sliced
40 g (1½ oz) raisins
400 ml (¾ pint) water
25 g (1 oz) creamed coconut
1 tablespoon lemon juice
salt and pepper
50 g (2 oz) toasted flaked almonds

Fry the onion in oil in a large saucepan for 10 minutes, then stir in the cinnamon and cook for a moment or two. Add beans, apricots, raisins and water, bring up to the boil, then turn heat down and leave to simmer, covered, for 15–20 minutes, until apricots are tender. Add coconut cream, lemon juice and seasoning. Sprinkle almonds on top before serving.

Butter Bean and Black Olive Dip

This tangy dip makes a refreshing starter. It is also good as a sandwich filling or spread for savoury biscuits or crisp toast triangles.

SERVES 4 (F)

125 g (4 oz) butter beans,
   cooked and drained,
   or 1 425 g (15 oz) can
12 black olives, stoned and
   mashed
2 tablespoons olive oil

2 tablespoons lemon juice
salt and pepper
tabasco
crisp lettuce leaves
chopped chives

Mash the beans, then add the olives, oil, lemon juice, salt and pepper and a drop or two of tabasco. Serve on individual plates on crisp lettuce leaves with some chives snipped over the top. Or treat as pâté, spoon into a small dish and serve with fingers of hot toast or melba toast.

Butter Beans with Tomatoes and Green Pepper

A delicious moist casserole in which the butter beans are flavoured with garlic, peppers and tomatoes. It's rich in protein and served with rice, noodles, bread or potatoes makes a complete meal.

SERVES 4 (F)

2 onions, chopped
25 g (1 oz) butter
2 garlic cloves, crushed
2 green peppers, sliced
450 g (1 lb) tomatoes, skinned
   and chopped, or 1 400 g
   (14 oz) can

1 tablespoon tomato purée
225 g (8 oz) butter beans, soaked
   and cooked
salt and pepper

Fry onions in the butter for 10 minutes, then add the garlic, peppers, tomatoes and tomato purée. Cover and cook for 15 minutes, stirring often. Add butter beans and season with salt and pepper. Cover and simmer gently for 10–15 minutes. Check seasoning and serve. For a special treat, this is delicious with some soured cream stirred into it just before serving; or with jacket potatoes filled with soured cream and chopped chives.

Cannellini Beans with Mushrooms and Soured Cream

This is very simple and quick to do and can be served as an accompanying vegetable or as a main course in its own right, with buttered noodles, warm bread or rice.

SERVES 4

225 g (8 oz) cannellini beans, soaked and cooked, or 2 425 g (15 oz) cans
175 g (6 oz) button mushrooms, wiped and sliced

25 g (1 oz) butter
½ teaspoon cornflour
300 ml (11 fl oz) soured cream
salt, pepper and grated nutmeg

Drain beans. Fry mushrooms in the butter for 3–4 minutes without browning, then add the cornflour. Cook for a few seconds, then add the soured cream, beans, and salt, pepper and nutmeg to taste. Heat gently, stirring all the time. Serve as soon as possible.

Chick Peas Fried in Garlic Butter

These chick peas make tasty cocktail nibbles or are delicious with tomato and onion in warm pitta bread. They also make a good first course, served hot on individual plates with a slice of lemon and a spoonful of mayonnaise.

SERVES 4 (F)

225 g (8 oz) chick peas, soaked
   and cooked, or 2 425 g
   (15 oz) cans
self-raising flour to coat

salt and pepper
50 g (2 oz) butter
2 tablespoons oil
2–4 garlic cloves, crushed

Drain the chick peas thoroughly. Spread them out on a large plate and sprinkle with the flour and a little salt and pepper. Turn them gently so that each one is coated with flour. Heat butter and oil in a large frying pan, add garlic and chick peas. Fry chick peas gently, until crisp, turning them often: you may need to do them in more than one batch. Serve at once.

Dal

Dal makes a good side dish with curries and is also good poured over lightly cooked root vegetables, turning them into a complete winter meal.

SERVES 4 (F)

225 g (8 oz) red lentils
850 ml (1½ pints) water
1 bay leaf
5 cm (2 in) piece cinnamon stick
4 cardamoms
2 teaspoons ground coriander
2 teaspoons ground cumin
4 tablespoons oil
2 onions, chopped
2 garlic cloves, crushed
1 tablespoon lemon juice
salt and pepper

Put lentils, water, bay leaf and cinnamon into a saucepan. Cook gently until lentils are tender: 20–25 minutes. Meanwhile fry spices in oil for 1–2 minutes, then add onion and garlic and fry for 10 minutes, until tender. Add this mixture, including the oil, to the cooked lentils, then stir in lemon juice and seasoning.

Felafel

These crisp little chick pea fritters are popular throughout the Middle East. Served Middle Eastern style, with salad in pitta bread, they make a filling and nutritious meal. You need a food processor or electric grater for this recipe.

SERVES 4 (F)

350 g (12 oz) chick peas, soaked
1 onion
2 garlic cloves, crushed
2 teaspoons ground coriander
2 teaspoons ground cumin

2 tablespoons flour
salt and pepper
extra flour to coat
oil for shallow-frying

Drain chick peas, then grind them, together with the onion and garlic, in a food processor or electric grater. Add spices, flour and seasoning. Mix well. Form into walnut-sized balls, then flatten to 6 mm (¼ in) and coat with flour. Fry slowly on both sides until outside is golden brown and crisp and inside is cooked. Drain and serve as soon as possible.

Field Bean Burgers

You can make these burgers for practically nothing and they are chewy, filling and delicious. But you do need a food processor or strong blender to break down the skins of the beans.

SERVES 4 Ⓕ

1 onion, chopped
2 tablespoons oil
2 garlic cloves, crushed
350 g (12 oz) field beans, soaked
    and cooked

4 tablespoons chopped parsley
1 tablespoon lemon juice
salt and pepper
flour to coat
oil for shallow-frying

Fry the onion in the oil for 5 minutes, then add the garlic and fry for a further 5 minutes. Chop beans in food processor until reduced to a coarse purée. Add onion, parsley, lemon juice and salt and pepper to taste. Coat with flour, then shallow-fry on both sides until crisp and browned. Drain on kitchen paper and serve immediately.

Field Bean Pâté

This is a coarse-textured pâté with a delicious earthy flavour. It's very economical and good as a light supper dish or first course, with fingers of hot wholewheat toast and a tomato salad, but you do need a food processor or strong blender to chop the beans.

SERVES 4 (F)

225 g (8 oz) field beans, soaked
  and cooked
2 garlic cloves, chopped
bunch of parsley

4 teaspoons wine vinegar
2 tablespoons olive oil
salt and pepper

Drain the beans, reserving liquid. Put beans, garlic, parsley, vinegar and oil into a food processor or blender and blend thoroughly to break down skins and make a coarse-textured purée. Add a little of the cooking liquid if necessary to make a consistency like thick whipped cream. Add salt and pepper to taste, then spoon mixture into a shallow pottery bowl or pâté dish.

Flageolet Cream Soup with Fresh Tarragon

A pale green soup that's equally good served hot or cold. If you're serving it cold, use 2 tablespoons oil instead of the butter. The fresh tarragon garnish is delicious if you can get it, but if not, chopped chives make a good substitute.

SERVES 4 (F)

25 g (1 oz) butter
1 onion, chopped
1 leek, sliced
125 g (4 oz) flageolet beans,
   soaked, rinsed and drained

850 ml (1½ pints) water or
   unsalted stock
4 tablespoons cream
salt and pepper
1 tablespoon chopped tarragon

Melt the butter in a large saucepan and fry the onion and leek gently for 10 minutes. Then add the flageolet beans and stir for a moment before adding the stock. Bring up to the boil, then simmer gently for about 1 hour, until beans are tender. Liquidize the soup, return to saucepan and stir in the cream. Season with salt and pepper. Reheat gently, but do not boil. Sprinkle some chopped tarragon over each bowlful.

Flageolet Beans in Avocados

These avocados, with their pale green filling of flageolet beans, make a good first course or light lunch with thin brown bread and butter.

SERVES 4

2 large avocados
75 g (3 oz) flageolet beans,
    cooked and drained
2 tablespoons chopped chives
4 teaspoons wine vinegar

4 tablespoons olive oil
salt and pepper
8 crisp lettuce leaves
4 sprigs watercress

Halve the avocados and remove stones, then carefully scoop out the flesh with a spoon, putting skins aside. Cut the flesh into even-sized pieces and put into a bowl with the flageolet beans and chives. Mix together the vinegar and oil, adding some salt and pepper to make a dressing. Pour this over avocado and beans and mix gently. Check seasoning. Put two lettuce leaves on each individual plate and place avocado skins on top. Divide bean mixture between skins, piling up well, and garnish with a sprig of watercress.

Haricot Bean Flan

Serve this tasty and filling flan hot with a crisp salad or lightly cooked vegetables.

SERVES 4 (F)

125 g (4 oz) wholewheat
  shortcrust pastry
1 onion, chopped
125 g (4 oz) haricot beans,
  soaked and cooked
25 g (1 oz) butter
125 g (4 oz) well-flavoured
  Cheddar cheese

1 egg
150 ml (¼ pint) creamy milk
1 teaspoon dry mustard
salt and pepper
2 tomatoes, sliced

Set oven to 200°C (400°F), gas mark 6. Roll out pastry and line a 20 cm (8 in) flan tin. Prick base and bake for 15–20 minutes. Fry onion in butter for 10 minutes then pour into hot flan case. Reduce oven setting to 180°C (350°F), gas mark 4. Drain beans thoroughly. Arrange beans and cheese evenly in flan. Whisk together the egg, milk, mustard and seasoning. Pour into flan, then arrange tomato slices on top. Bake for 35–40 minutes, until set.

Hummus

Hummus is delicious served with warm wholewheat pitta bread, which you break off and use to scoop up the hummus. It's an excellent first course, particularly before a vegetable casserole, but is a nourishing and irresistible snack any time! Tahini, or sesame cream, can be bought from health shops but omit it if necessary: the hummus will still be very good.

SERVES 4 (F)

125 g (4 oz) chick peas, soaked
   and cooked
1 garlic clove, crushed
1 tablespoon olive oil
2 teaspoons tahini

2–3 teaspoons lemon juice
salt and pepper
extra olive oil, paprika and
   lemon wedges to serve

Drain chick peas, reserving liquid. Liquidize chick peas with garlic, oil, tahini, lemon juice and enough of the liquid to make a purée about the consistency of lightly whipped cream. Season. Divide between four flat plates, spreading out the hummus to a depth of 1 cm (½ in). Indent top lightly with prongs of fork. Pour a little olive oil over the top, sprinkle with paprika and garnish with lemon wedges.

Khitchari

Serve this Indian dish with poppadums and a tomato and onion salad.

SERVES 4–6 Ⓕ

1 onion, chopped
4 garlic cloves, crushed
1 teaspoon turmeric powder
1 teaspoon grated ginger root
½ teaspoon curry powder
1 teaspoon ground cumin
3 tablespoons oil
175 g (6 oz) potato, peeled and
  cut into chunks

225 g (8 oz) mung beans,
  soaked, rinsed and drained
225 g (8 oz) brown rice
1 litre (1¾ pints) water
2 tablespoons lemon juice
salt and pepper

Fry onion, garlic and spices in the oil for 10 minutes. Stir in potato, beans and rice, then add water and bring to boil. Cover and cook gently for 45 minutes. Turn off heat and leave to stand for 15 minutes, until liquid has been absorbed. Add lemon juice and seasoning.

Lentil and Cheese Slice

A simple, quick-to-make supper dish which children like: crisp golden lentil and cheese slices. Serve with parsley sauce, new potatoes and a green vegetable. They're also good cold, with pickles and salad.

SERVES 4 (F)

225 g (8 oz) split red lentils
1 onion, sliced
1 bay leaf
450 ml (16 fl oz) water

50 g (2 oz) grated cheese
salt and pepper
1 tomato, thinly sliced
a little soft margarine

Put lentils, onion and bay leaf into a saucepan with the water and cook gently, without a lid, for 20–25 minutes, until lentils are tender. Remove bay leaf. Set oven to 220°C (425°F), gas mark 7. Beat half the cheese into the cooked lentils and season. Grease a 20 cm (8 in) square tin, spoon in lentil mixture, spreading to corners. Top with remaining cheese and tomato slices, dot with margarine. Bake for 20–25 minutes.

Curried Lentil and Apple Soup

This is a delectable soup which can be served hot or chilled. I think it's especially good chilled with a little cream on top.

SERVES 4 (F)

25 g (1 oz) butter
1 onion, chopped
1 carrot, scraped and chopped
125 g (4 oz) cooking apple,
    peeled and chopped
2 teaspoons curry powder

175 g (6 oz) red lentils
1 bay leaf
850 ml (1½ pints) water or stock
1 tablespoon lemon juice
salt and pepper

Heat the butter in a large saucepan and fry the onion, carrot, apple and curry powder for 10 minutes, without browning. Then stir in the lentils, bay leaf and stock or water. Bring up to the boil, then simmer gently for 20–30 minutes, until lentils and vegetables are cooked. Remove bay leaf. Liquidize soup, then return to saucepan, add lemon juice and season. Reheat, or chill before serving.

Lentils with Coriander and Fresh Ginger

A simple dish with a delicious spicy flavour. Serve with fluffy cooked rice, mango chutney and crisp poppadums.

SERVES 4–6 (F)

2 onions, chopped
3 tablespoons oil
2 bay leaves
2 garlic cloves, crushed
4 teaspoons ground coriander
1 tablespoon grated fresh ginger

450 g (1 lb) continental or puy lentils, soaked, cooked and drained
salt and pepper
3 tomatoes, sliced

Fry onions in the oil with the bay leaf for 5 minutes, then add garlic, coriander and ginger and fry for a further 5 minutes. Add drained lentils, mix well, season. Heat gently, stirring often, until piping hot, then remove bay leaves, pile lentils into a hot dish and arrange the sliced tomatoes all round the edge.

Lentil and Parsley Spread

This spread makes a good protein-rich sandwich filling or topping for fingers of toast or savoury biscuits.

SERVES 4 Ⓕ

125 g (4 oz) red lentils
200 ml (7 fl oz) water
50 g (2 oz) butter
2 tablespoons chopped parsley

bunch of spring onions, chopped
pinch of chilli powder
1 tablespoon lemon juice
salt and pepper

Put the lentils into a pan with the water and cook gently until lentils are tender and water absorbed: 20–25 minutes. Beat butter into the lentils, together with parsley, spring onions, chilli, lemon juice and seasoning. Mix well to make a fairly creamy paste. Add a little water if necessary to achieve a spreading consistency.

Lentil Rissoles
in Chilli-tomato Sauce

SERVES 4 (F)

225 g (8 oz) red lentils
300 ml (½ pint) water
1 onion, chopped
2 tablespoons oil
1 tablespoon lemon juice

1 egg, beaten
salt and pepper
wholewheat flour to coat
oil for shallow-frying

For the sauce
1 onion, chopped
½ teaspoon chilli powder

2 tablespoons oil
1 425 g (15 oz) can tomatoes

Put lentils into a pan with the water and cook gently, uncovered, until lentils are tender and water absorbed: 20–25 minutes. Fry onion in oil for 10 minutes. Add onion, lemon juice, egg and seasoning to lentils, mix well. Cool, then form into rissoles, coat in flour and shallow-fry. To make sauce, fry onion and chilli powder in oil for 10 minutes. Add tomatoes, then liquidize. Season, then reheat and serve with the rissoles.

Lentil and Root Vegetable Stew

An economical and warming winter dish.

SERVES 4 (F)

3 onions, chopped
4 tablespoons oil
700 g (1½ lb) mixed root
  vegetables
2 sticks celery, sliced
2 garlic cloves, crushed
4 tomatoes, skinned and
  chopped

175 g (6 oz) red lentils
850 ml (1½ pints) unsalted stock
  or water
2 teaspoons ground coriander
2 teaspoons ground cumin
1 tablespoon lemon juice
salt and pepper

Fry half the onion in half the oil for 5 minutes; add rest of vegetables, garlic and lentils. Fry for a further 5 minutes, stirring often. Then add stock or water and simmer gently, uncovered, until lentils and vegetables are tender: about 30 minutes. Meanwhile, fry rest of onion, coriander and cumin in remaining oil for 10 minutes. Add to lentil mixture, along with lemon juice and seasoning. Serve with baked potatoes or cooked rice.

Pea Soup with Mint

This is cheap, warming and easy to make. Fresh mint gives a delicious flavour, but if you can't get it, flavour with a little mint sauce concentrate at the end of the cooking time.

SERVES 4–6 (F)

1 onion, chopped
25 g (1 oz) butter
225 g (8 oz) whole dried peas, soaked for 6–8 hours, drained and rinsed
1.7 litre (3 pints) water or unsalted stock

small bunch mint, stalks removed
salt, pepper and sugar
lemon juice

Fry the onion in the butter, without browning, for 10 minutes, then add the peas and water. Bring to the boil, then cover and simmer very gently for about 2 hours, until the peas are soft. Add the mint, then liquidize. Return to saucepan; season to taste with salt, pepper, a little sugar and lemon juice.

Pease Pudding

Originally cooked in a floured cloth and served to eke out expensive meat, I like to cook pease pudding in a bowl and serve it with crisp roast potatoes, mint sauce and a green vegetable.

SERVES 4 (F)

225g (8 oz) yellow split peas
1 large onion, chopped
50 g (2 oz) butter

1 egg
salt and pepper

Cook the split peas in plenty of water until tender, then drain. Meanwhile fry onion in the butter for 10 minutes. Add onion to the peas, then beat in the egg and season to taste. Turn mixture into a buttered bowl, cover with foil and steam for 1 hour. Or bake the mixture in a greased casserole dish in a moderate oven 180°C (350°F), gas mark 4 for 30–40 minutes.

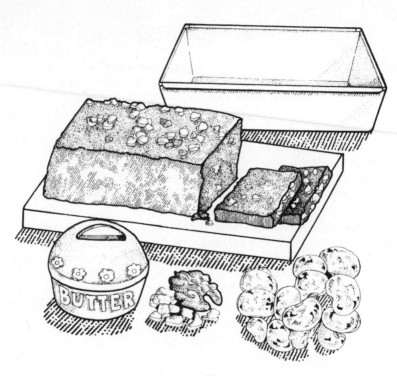

Sweet Pinto Bean Tea Bread

The Texan girl who sent me the idea for this bread says she finds it useful for breakfast, 'easily grabbed on the way out the door'. It also makes a nourishing after-school snack.

MAKES ONE 450 G (1 LB) LOAF Ⓕ

75 g (3 oz) pinto beans
200 g (7 oz) self-raising flour
½ teaspoon cinnamon
½ teaspoon mixed spice
50 g (2 oz) margarine

50 g (2 oz) dark brown sugar
75 g (3 oz) golden syrup
1 egg, beaten
75 g (3 oz) chopped walnuts

Soak pinto beans, then boil for 1¼–1½ hours until tender; drain and mash. Set oven to 180°C (350°F), gas mark 4. Grease and line a 450 g (1 lb) loaf tin. Sift dry ingredients into a bowl. Heat margarine, sugar and syrup until melted. Cool to lukewarm, then add dry ingredients together with egg, beans and two-thirds of nuts. Spoon into tin, sprinkle with rest of nuts, bake for 1 hour. Cool on wire rack. Serve sliced and buttered.

Quick and Easy Red Bean and Tomato Pie

SERVES 4

750 g (1½ lb) potatoes, peeled
   and cut into chunks
salt
40 g (1½ oz) butter or margarine
a little milk
125 g (4 oz) grated cheese
freshly ground black pepper
1 onion, chopped

1 425 g (15 oz) can tomatoes
1 425 g (15 oz) can red kidney
   beans, drained, or 125 g (4 oz)
   red kidney beans, soaked,
   cooked and drained

Set oven to 200°C (400°F), gas mark 6, or prepare a hot grill. Cook potatoes in salted water to cover until tender, then drain and mash with half the butter or margarine, cheese and milk to make a soft consistency. Season. While potatoes are cooking, fry the onion in remaining butter or margarine, then add tomatoes and beans, mashing them a little. Spoon red bean mixture into a shallow, greased, ovenproof dish, spread potato on top and sprinkle with remaining cheese. Bake for 25–30 minutes. Or have bean mixture and potatoes piping hot when you put them in the dish, then just brown the top under the grill.

Red Beans with Rice and Vegetables

Golden rice flecked with red kidney beans and green, red and orange vegetables. Serve with a green salad.

SERVES 4 (F)

2 onions, chopped
2 garlic cloves, crushed
4 tablespoons oil
350 g (12 oz) brown rice
1 tablespoon turmeric powder
850 ml (1½ pints) water
salt and pepper
4 carrots, diced

2 courgettes, sliced
1 red pepper, deseeded and
  chopped
4 tomatoes, skinned and
  chopped
125 g (4 oz) red kidney beans,
  cooked

Fry onion and garlic in oil for 10 minutes, then stir in rice and turmeric. Add water and seasoning, bring to boil, cover and simmer for 20 minutes. Then add carrot – don't stir in. Ten minutes later add rest of vegetables and beans; again, don't stir in. Cook for further 10 minutes (40 minutes in all), then remove from heat and leave to stand for 15 minutes. Mix gently with a fork; check seasoning.

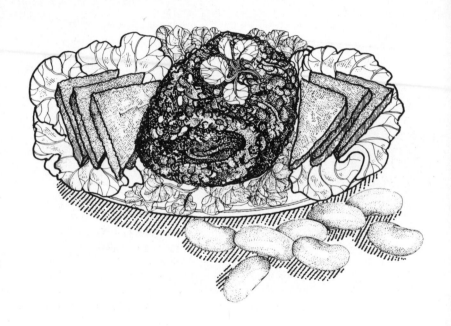

Refried Red Beans

This traditional South American dish, *frijoles refritos*, is good with crisp toast triangles and a lettuce and watercress salad. If you use canned beans, it makes a good emergency meal.

SERVES 4 (F)

2 onions, chopped
2 garlic cloves, crushed
3 tablespoons oil
40 g (1½ oz) butter
225 g (8 oz) red kidney beans,
   soaked and cooked, or 2 425 g
   (15 oz) cans

¼–½ teaspoon chilli powder
salt and pepper
triangles of toast to serve

Fry the onions and garlic in half the oil and butter for 10 minutes. Then add the remaining oil and butter and the beans, mashing them with a fork and mixing them with the onions and garlic, and the chilli powder, salt and pepper to taste. Continue to fry the beans for 10–15 minutes, until they form a 'cake' with a crisp base, rather like a large potato cake. Then flip over one side to form a roll. Serve immediately.

Soupe au Pistou

This delicious soup from southern France makes a filling main course with warm crusty bread.

SERVES 6 (F)

2 onions, chopped
7 tablespoons olive oil
225 g (8 oz) haricot beans, cooked
2 carrots, chopped
2 potatoes, peeled and diced
225 g (8 oz) courgettes, sliced
125 g (4 oz) green beans, sliced

450 g (1 lb) tomatoes, peeled and chopped
1.7 litre (3 pints) unsalted stock or water
50 g (2 oz) vermicelli
salt and pepper
5 cloves garlic, crushed
leaves from a bunch of basil

Fry onion in 3 tablespoons of oil for 5 minutes. Add haricot beans and vegetables and cook for 5 minutes. Pour in stock, simmer for 20–30 minutes. Then add vermicelli and cook for 10 minutes. Season. Liquidize remaining oil, garlic and basil; stir into soup just before serving or put into a bowl for people to add themselves.

Green Split Pea Loaf with Carrot and Mint

A cheap and tasty non-meat loaf, this is prettily flecked with pieces of orange carrot and dark green mint.

SERVES 4 (F)

250 g (9 oz) green split peas
1 onion, chopped
1 carrot, chopped
1 garlic clove, crushed
25 g (1 oz) butter

½ teaspoon marjoram
2 tablespoons chopped mint
1 egg, beaten
salt and pepper

Put split peas into a pan, cover with water and boil gently until tender: 40–60 minutes. Drain. Set oven to 190°C (375°F), gas mark 5. Grease a 450 g (1 lb) loaf tin and line with a strip of greased silicone paper. Fry onion, carrot and garlic in the butter for 10 minutes. Add to drained peas, together with marjoram, mint, egg and plenty of seasoning. Spoon into tin, cover with foil and bake for 40–45 minutes. To serve, turn out on to a warmed dish and cut into thick slices.

Split Green Peas
with Cream and Leeks

A substantial yet elegant vegetable dish: delicious with the garnish of fresh mint if you can get it.

SERVES 4

175 g (6 oz) split green peas
400 ml (¾ pint) water
25 g (1 oz) butter
salt and pepper

1 kg (2¼ lb) leeks
4 tablespoons single cream
1–2 tablespoons chopped mint,
    if available

Put the peas into a saucepan with the water and simmer gently until very tender: 50–60 minutes. Liquidize, adding more water if necessary to make a soft consistency, like lightly whipped cream. Then add half the butter and season to taste. Meanwhile trim and wash the leeks and cut them into 2.5 cm (1 in) lengths. Cook leeks in a little boiling water until just tender; drain very well and add remaining butter and some seasoning. Spoon leeks into a warmed serving dish, pour the split green pea sauce on top, and the cream and chopped mint on top of that. Serve at once.

Split Peas with Fennel Seeds and Hardboiled Eggs

A simple mixture with a distinctive flavour. Serve it as a vegetable accompaniment, or with triangles of toast and a green salad for an economical supper.

SERVES 4

350 g (12 oz) yellow split peas
2 onions, chopped
50 g (2 oz) butter
1–2 tablespoons lemon juice

salt and pepper
1 tablespoon fennel seeds
3 hardboiled eggs, quartered

Cook the peas in plenty of water until tender – 45–50 minutes – then drain. Meanwhile fry the onion in half the butter until softened and lightly browned: 10 minutes. Add this to the cooked peas, mixing well to mash the peas a little. Add the lemon juice and season with salt and pepper. Spoon mixture into a shallow serving dish and keep it warm. Melt remaining butter and fry the fennel seeds for 1–2 minutes, until they start to pop, then pour the seeds and butter over the top of the split pea mixture, tuck the hardboiled egg quarters round the edge and serve as soon as possible.

Tomatoes Stuffed with Cannellini Beans, Spring Onions and Mayonnaise

Serve this pretty dish with thinly sliced brown bread and butter as a refreshing starter, or make it the centrepiece of a cold lunch or supper, with crisp lettuce, cucumber and grated carrot. Use large tomatoes, but not the very big ones.

SERVES 2–4

4 good-sized tomatoes
salt
75 g (3 oz) cannellini beans,
   cooked and drained
2 tablespoons mayonnaise

2 tablespoons natural yoghurt
6 spring onions, chopped
pepper
4 crisp lettuce leaves

Slice tops off tomatoes and scoop out seeds. Sprinkle inside of tomatoes with salt and leave upside down to drain. Put beans into a bowl and add mayonnaise, yoghurt and spring onions. Mix gently; season to taste. Put a crisp lettuce leaf on each serving dish and stand a tomato on top. Spoon bean mixture into tomatoes.

Yellow and Green Split Pea Salad with Lemon and Mint

An attractive mixture of colours, this salad is best if you undercook the split peas a little so that they retain their shape and have a slightly chewy texture.

SERVES 4 (F)

125 g (4 oz) yellow split peas
125 g (4 oz) green split peas
½ teaspoon dry mustard
½ teaspoon sugar

grated rind and juice of 1 lemon
4 tablespoons olive oil
2 tablespoons chopped mint
salt and pepper

Cook the split peas in separate pans, in plenty of water, until just tender: 30–40 minutes. Drain well. Meanwhile put the mustard, sugar, lemon rind and juice and oil into a large bowl and mix together. Add the split peas and mint, season to taste and mix gently. Cool, then transfer to a serving dish.

Index

Once upon a time...

...a big bad wolf was roaming hungrily through a forest. One day, he saw a basket lying on the ground, and his greedy eyes peered around...

LITTLE RED RIDING HOOD

Once upon a time... in the middle of a thick forest stood a small cottage, the home of a pretty little girl known to everyone as Little Red Riding Hood. One day, her Mummy waved her goodbye at the garden gate, saying: "Grandma is ill. Take her this basket of cakes, but be very careful. Keep to the path through the woods and don't stop. That way, you will come to no harm."

"Don't worry," said Little Red Riding Hood, "I'll run all the way to Grandma's without stopping."

The little girl made her way through the woods, but she was soon to forget her mother's words.

"What lovely strawberries! And so red..."

Laying her basket on the ground, Little Red Riding Hood bent over the strawberry plants. "They're nice and ripe, and so big! Yummy!"

Little Red Riding Hood ran back and forth popping strawberries into her mouth. Suddenly she remembered Grandma and the basket... and hurried back towards the path. The basket was still in the grass and, humming to herself, Little Red Riding Hood walked on.

The woods became thicker and thicker. Suddenly she saw some large daisies in the grass.

"Oh, how sweet!" she exclaimed and, thinking of Grandma, she picked a large bunch of flowers.

In the meantime, two wicked eyes were spying on her from behind a tree... a strange rustling in the woods made Little Red Riding Hood's heart thump.

Suddenly, she heard the sound of a gruff voice which said: "Where are you going, my pretty girl, all alone in the woods?"

"I'm taking Grandma some cakes," said Little Red Riding Hood, in a trembling voice.

The big bad wolf asked: "Does Grandma live by herself?"

"Oh, yes," replied Little Red Riding Hood, "and she never opens the door to strangers!"

"Goodbye. Perhaps we'll meet again," replied the wolf. Then he loped away thinking to himself, "I'll gobble the grandmother first, then lie in wait for the grandchild!" At last, the cottage came in sight. The wolf rapped on the door.

"Who's there?" cried Grandma from her bed.

"It's me, Little Red Riding Hood. I've brought you some cakes," replied the wolf, trying to hide his gruff voice.

"Come in," said Grandma. A horrible shadow appeared on the wall. Poor Grandma! In one bound, the wolf leapt across the room and, in a single mouthful, swallowed the old lady. Soon after, Little Red Riding Hood tapped on the door.

"Grandma, can I come in?" she called.

Now, the wolf had put on the old lady's shawl and cap and slipped into the bed. Trying to imitate Grandma's quavering little voice, he replied: "Open the latch and come in!"

"What a deep voice you have," said the little girl in surprise.

"The better to greet you with," said the wolf.

"Goodness, what big eyes you have."

"The better to see you with."

"And what big hands you have!" exclaimed Little Red Riding Hood.

"The better to hug you with," said the wolf.

"What a big mouth you have," the little girl murmured.

"The better to eat you with!" growled the wolf, and jumping out of bed, he swallowed her up too. Then, with a fat full tummy, he fell fast asleep.

In the meantime, a hunter passing by the cottage, decided to stop and ask for a drink. He had spent a lot of time trying to catch a large wolf, but had lost its tracks. The hunter could hear a strange whistling sound coming from inside the cottage.

He peered through the window... and saw the large wolf, with a fat full tummy, snoring away in Grandma's bed.

"The wolf! He won't get away this time!"

Without making a sound, the hunter loaded his gun and opened the window. He pointed the barrel straight at the wolf's head and... BANG! The wolf was dead.

"Got you at last!" shouted the hunter. "You'll never frighten anyone again."

He cut open the wolf's stomach and to his amazement, out popped Grandma and Little Red Riding Hood, safe and unharmed.

"You arrived just in time," murmured the old lady.

"It's safe to go home now," the hunter told Little Red Riding Hood. "The big bad wolf is dead and gone, and there is no danger on the path."

Much later, Little Red Riding Hood's mother arrived, worried because her little girl had not come home. When she saw Little Red Riding Hood, safe and sound, she burst into tears of joy.

After thanking the hunter again, Little Red Riding Hood and her mother set off towards home. As they walked quickly through the woods, the little girl told her mother: "We must always keep to the path and never stop. That way, we'll come to no harm!"

THE UGLY DUCKLING

Once upon a time... down on a farm, lived a duck family. Mother Duck had been sitting on some new eggs. One nice morning, the eggs hatched and out popped six ducklings. But one egg was bigger than the rest, and it didn't hatch. Mother Duck couldn't recall laying that seventh egg. How did it get there?

But before she had time to think about it, the last egg finally hatched. A strange looking duckling with grey feathers, that should have been yellow, gazed at Mother Duck.

"I can't understand how this ugly duckling can be one of mine!" she said to herself, shaking her head. The grey duckling wasn't pretty, and since he ate far more than his brothers, he was outgrowing them. As the days went by, the poor ugly duckling became more and more unhappy.

His brothers didn't want to play with him, he was so clumsy, and all the farmyard folks laughed at him. He felt sad and lonely.

"Poor little ugly duckling!" Mother Duck would say. "Why are you so different from the others?" The ugly duckling felt worse and worse.

"Nobody loves me, they all tease me!" Then one day, at sunrise, he ran away from the farmyard.

He stopped at a pond and began to question all the other birds: "Do you know of any ducklings with grey feathers like mine?" But everyone shook their heads.

"We don't know anyone as ugly as you." He went to another pond, where a pair of large geese gave him the same answer to his question. What's more, they warned him: "Don't stay here! It's dangerous. There are men with guns around here!"

Then one day, he came to an old woman's cottage. Thinking he was a goose, she caught him and put him in a cage.

"I hope it lays plenty of eggs!" said the old woman. But the ugly duckling laid not a single egg. The hen kept frightening him:

"If you don't lay eggs, the old woman will wring your neck and pop you into the pot!" And the cat chipped in: "Hee! Hee! I hope the woman cooks you soon, then I can gnaw at your bones!" The poor ugly duckling was so scared that he lost his appetite, though the old woman kept stuffing him with food and grumbling: "If you won't lay eggs, at least hurry up and get plump!"

"Oh, dear me!" moaned the terrified duckling. "I'll die of fright first!"

Then one night, finding the cage door ajar, he escaped. At dawn, he found himself in a thick bed of reeds. There was plenty of food, and the duckling began to feel a little happier, though he was lonely. One day at sunrise, he saw a flight of beautiful birds wing overhead. White, with long slender necks, yellow beaks and large wings, they were migrating south.

"If only I could look like them!" said the duckling.

Winter came and the water in the reed bed froze. The poor duckling left to seek food in the snow. He dropped exhausted to the ground, but a farmer found him.

"I'll take him home to my children. They'll look after him."

The duckling was showered with kindly care at the farmer's house.

14

By springtime, he had grown so big that the farmer decided: "I'll set him free by the pond!" That was when the duckling saw himself mirrored in the water.

"Goodness! How I've changed! I hardly recognize myself!"

The flight of swans winged north again and glided on to the pond.

When the duckling saw them, he realized he was one of their kind, and soon made friends.

One day, as he swam majestically with his fellow swans, he heard children on the river bank exclaim: "Look at that young swan! He's the finest of them all!"

And he almost burst with happiness.

THE OBSTINATE GOATS

Once upon a time... two mountain goats happened to be going down the opposite slopes of a valley, through which flowed a rushing river.

The mountain dwellers had bridged the river by placing a large tree trunk to join the steep rocky banks.

The two goats met head on half way across the tree trunk, for each wanted to cross to the other side. But the trunk was not wide enough for them to pass each other, and neither goat wanted to give way.

They began to bicker, but neither would budge an inch. Words soon led to action and they started to fight, till finally both tumbled off the tree trunk into the river below.

Wouldn't it have been much simpler if one of the goats had been courteous enough to allow the other to pass?

© DAMI EDITORE, ITALY
PUBLISHED BY
MADISON MARKETING LIMITED
110 Eglinton Avenue East
Toronto, ON   M4P 2Y1

In conjunction with
TORMONT PUBLICATIONS INC.
338 St. Antoine St. East
Montreal, PQ   H2Y 1A3

Madison Marketing Limited
holds the exclusive license
to this edition.
ISBN 2-89429-150-7
ITEM M13-17

Graphic Design and Layout: Zapp
Illustrations: Tony Wolf, Piero Cattaneo
Text: Peter Holeinone
Adaptation: Angela Rahaniotis
PRINTED IN CANADA